Heaven's Heroes
One Smooth Stone

PEOPLE ARE TALKING ABOUT *One Smooth Stone*

As a Family pastor, I'm always looking for resources that help parents convey God's word to their children in a way that's easy to understand. *One Smooth Stone* is repetitive and rhythmic so that every young child can remember it, and it's beautifully illustrated to keep even the youngest children's attention.
—**Kurt Brodback**, Family Ministry Pastor, Northview Church

This book will have great appeal for young readers and for those who listen to its message. As each page builds on the last, repetition solidifies the learning of God's word. A very creative way to teach children God's precious word.
—**Lora Pettigrew-Goff**, Retired Elementary Educator, Author of "Growing Up With Granny"

After her first publication of *The Squirrel Family Acorn* based on the Bible verse James 1:17, Kristin Lehr once again uses her God-given gift of creativity, Bible knowledge, and ability to communicate the word of God to children in a repetitive fun way. In her latest book, *One Smooth Stone*, Kristin reinforces God's word by telling the story of David and Goliath. Through reading *One Smooth Stone*, children will be encouraged to be bold in their faith like the shepherd boy in the story. I love Kristin's unique writing style and ability to make God's word relatable and come alive. God's message is made simple in this story of boldness and faith. Kristin writes in a way that helps readers see clearly the message they can apply in their daily lives through each of her books. One Smooth Stone is a story that has the potential to shape a child's faith and a love for God's word.
—**Lisa Cox**, Author of *Not Yet* and *Grit, Not Grits*

HEAVEN'S HEROES
One Smooth Stone

Kristin Lehr
Illustrated by Alicia Berry

PUBLISHING THE POSITIVE
ELK LAKE PUBLISHING INC
Plymouth, Massachusetts

Cover and Interior Design: Derinda Babcock
Editor(s): Derinda Babcock, Deb Haggerty
Illustrated by: Alicia Berry
Author Represented by WordWise Media

PUBLISHED BY: Elk Lake Publishing, Inc., 35 Dogwood Dr., Plymouth, MA 02360, 2019

Library Cataloging Data
Names: Lehr, Kristin (Kristin Lehr)
One Smooth Stone / Kristin Lehr
42 p. 21.6 cm × 21.6 cm (8.5 in × 8.5 in.)

Description: *One Smooth Stone* is the exciting retelling of the epic biblical battle of David and Goliath. In addition, each page ends with Scripture so children can easily understand that when we are the underdog, our power comes from God.

Identifiers: ISBN-13: 978-1-950051-53-3 (trade) | 978-1-950051-54-0 (POD) | 978-1-950051-55-7 (e-book)

Key Words: Bible stories, David, Goliath, inspiration, children, early childhood learning
LCCN: 2019xxxxxx Nonfiction

Author's Dedication

Chip,
I love you and I like you. ❤️

This is one smooth stone.

Thank you, God, for making me bold and strong.

This is the river that polishes one smooth stone.

Thank you, God, for making me bold and strong.

These are the ripples that flow through the river that polishes one smooth stone.

Thank you, God, for making me bold and strong.

This is the hill above the ripples
that flow through the river
that polishes one smooth stone.

Thank you, God, for making me bold and strong.

This is the sun that shines on the hill
above the ripples that flow through the river
that polishes one smooth stone.

Thank you, God, for making me bold and strong.

This is the army that stands in the sun
that shines on the hill above the ripples
that flow through the river
that polishes one smooth stone.

Thank you, God, for making me bold and strong.

This is a giant who fights for the army
that stands in the sun
that shines on the hill above the ripples
that flow through the river
that polishes one smooth stone.

Thank you, God, for making me bold and strong.

His name is Goliath, the really big giant
who fights for the army
that stands in the sun
that shines on the hill above the ripples
that flow through the river
that polishes one smooth stone.

Thank you, God, for making me bold and strong.

These are God's people who shake in their boots
when seeing Goliath, the really big giant,
who fights for the army that stands in the sun
that shines on the hill above the ripples
that flow through the river
that polishes one smooth stone.

Thank you, God, for making me bold and strong.

This is the king who rules God's people
who shake in their boots
when seeing Goliath, the really big giant,
who fights for the army that stands in the sun
that shines on the hill above the ripples
that flow through the river
that polishes one smooth stone.

Thank you, God, for making me bold and strong.

This is a sheep-herding boy, a chosen boy,
who serves the king who rules God's people
who shake in their boots when seeing Goliath,
the really big giant, who fights for the army
that stands in the sun
that shines on the hill above the ripples
that flow through the river
that polishes one smooth stone.

Thank you, God, for making me bold and strong.

Here is a slingshot pulled from the pocket
of a sheep-herding boy, a chosen boy,
who serves the king who rules God's people
who shake in their boots when seeing Goliath,
the really big giant, who fights for the army
that stands in the sun
that shines on the hill above the ripples
that flow through the river
that polishes one smooth stone.

Thank you, God, for making me bold and strong.

Whoosh goes the slingshot, a stone in the air,
pulled from the pocket
of a sheep-herding boy, a chosen boy,
who serves the king who rules God's people
who shake in their boots when seeing Goliath,
the really big giant, who fights for the army
that stands in the sun
that shines on the hill above the ripples
that flow through the river
that polishes one smooth stone.

Thank you, God, for making me bold and strong.

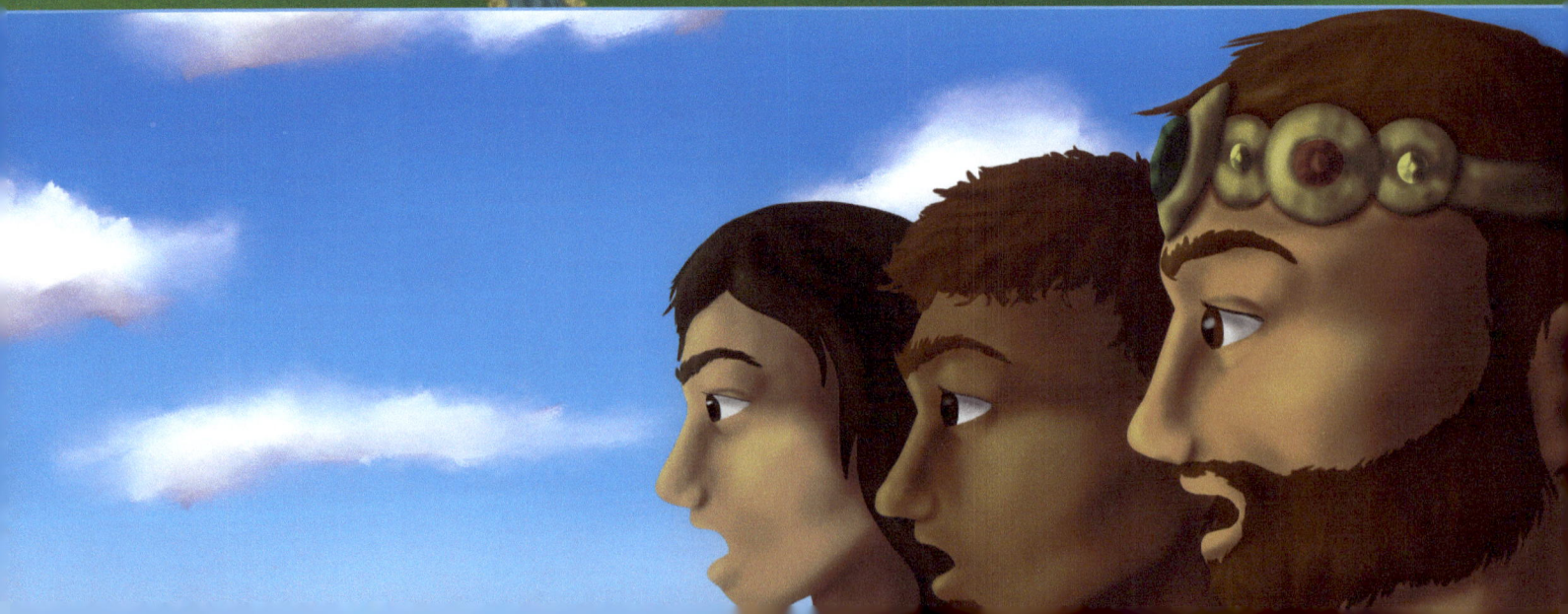

This is the silence while both armies stare
as **whoosh** goes the slingshot, a stone in the air,
pulled from the pocket
of a sheep-herding boy, a chosen boy,
who serves the king who rules God's people
who shake in their boots when seeing Goliath,
the really big giant, who fights for the army
that stands in the sun
that shines on the hill above the ripples
that flow through the river
that polishes one smooth stone.

Thank you, God, for making me bold and strong.

Down goes the giant after the silence
while both armies stare
as **whoosh** goes the slingshot, a stone in the air,
pulled from the pocket
of a sheep-herding boy, a chosen boy,
who serves the king who rules God's people
who shake in their boots when seeing Goliath,
the really big giant, who fights for the army
that stands in the sun
that shines on the hill above the ripples
that flow through the river
that polishes one smooth stone.

Thank you, God, for making me bold and strong.

These are God's people who send up a **CHEER**
for all those to hear
as down goes the giant after the silence
while both armies stare
as *whoosh* goes the slingshot, a stone in the air,
pulled from the pocket
of a sheep-herding boy, a chosen boy,
who serves the king who rules God's people
who shake in their boots when seeing Goliath,
the really big giant, who fights for the army
that stands in the sun
that shines on the hill above the ripples
that flow through the river that polishes one smooth
stone.

Thank you, God, for making me bold and strong.
Inspired from Joshua 1:9

ABOUT THE AUTHOR

DR. KRISTIN LEHR, author of *The Squirrel Family Acorn*, lives in Indiana with her husband and three sons. Her favorite thing is to spend time with family and friends. Her guilty pleasures are shopping and watching reality TV. Kristin enjoys a wonderful career as the Director of Children's Ministry at Zionsville Presbyterian Church in Zionsville, Indiana.

Stay tuned for the next exciting book in the *Heaven's Heroes* series…"

www.ingramcontent.com/pod-product-compliance
Lightning Source LLC
Chambersburg PA
CBHW042101040426
42448CB00002B/96